THE ESSENTIAL BRENDAN KENNELLY

Brendan Kennelly was born in 1936 in Ballylongford, Co. Kerry, and was Professor of Modern Literature at Trinity College, Dublin from 1973 until his retirement in 2005. He has published more than 30 books of poetry, including *Familiar Strangers: New & Selected Poems 1960-2004* (2004), which includes the whole of his book-length poem *The Man Made of Rain* (1998). He is best-known for two controversial poetry books, *Cromwell*, published in Ireland in 1983 and in Britain by Bloodaxe in 1987, and his epic poem *The Book of Judas* (1991), which topped the Irish bestsellers list: a shorter version was published by Bloodaxe in 2002 as *The Little Book of Judas*. His third epic, *Poetry My Arse* (1995), did much to outdo these in notoriety. All these remain available separately from Bloodaxe, along with his more recent titles: *Glimpses* (2001), *Martial Art* (2003), *Now* (2006); *Reservoir Voices* (2009), and *The Essential Brendan Kennelly: Selected Poems*, edited by Terence Brown and Michael Longley (2011).

His drama titles include *When Then Is Now* (2006), a trilogy of his modern versions of three Greek tragedies (all previously published by Bloodaxe): Sophocles' *Antigone* and Euripides' *Medea* and *The Trojan Women*. His *Antigone* and *The Trojan Women* were both first performed at the Peacock Theatre, Dublin, in 1986 and 1993 respectively; *Medea* premièred in the Dublin Theatre Festival in 1988, toured in England in 1989 and was broadcast by BBC Radio 3. His other plays include Lorca's *Blood Wedding* (Northern Stage, Newcastle & Bloodaxe, 1996).

His translations of Irish poetry are available in *Love of Ireland: Poems from the Irish* (Mercier Press, 1989). He has edited several anthologies, including *The Penguin Book of Irish Verse* (1970/1981), *Between Innocence and Peace: Favourite Poems of Ireland* (Mercier Press, 1993), *Ireland's Women: Writings Past and Present*, with Katie Donovan and A. Norman Jeffares (Gill & Macmillan, 1994), and *Dublines*, with Katie Donovan (Bloodaxe Books, 1995). He has also published two novels, *The Crooked Cross* (1963) and *The Florentines* (1967).

His *Journey into Joy: Selected Prose*, edited by Åke Persson, was published by Bloodaxe in 1994, along with *Dark Fathers into Light*, a critical anthology on his work edited by Richard Pine. John McDonagh's critical study *Brendan Kennelly: A Host of Ghosts* was published in The Liffey Press's Contemporary Irish Writers series in 2004.

He has also recorded a poetry CD, *Brendan Kennelly reading from his poems* (The Poetry Archive, 2002).

THE ESSENTIAL
BRENDAN KENNELLY
SELECTED POEMS

EDITED BY **TERENCE BROWN**
& **MICHAEL LONGLEY**

WITH CD OF POEMS READ BY
BRENDAN KENNELLY

WAKE FOREST UNIVERSITY PRESS

Wake Forest University Press

First North American edition published 2011

Copyright © 2011 by Brendan Kennelly

Introduction & selection © 2011 by

Terence Brown and Michael Longley

All rights reserved

For permission, required to reprint these poems, write to:

Wake Forest University Press

Post Office Box 7333, Winston-Salem, NC 27109

www.wfu.edu/wfupress

LCCN 2011938546

ISBN 978-1-930630-57-4 (paperback with CD)

Publication of this book has been aided by

the generosity of the Esseesse family

First published in the U.K. in 2011 by Bloodaxe Books

First printing

CONTENTS

from **THE BOOK OF JUDAS** (1991)

FOREWORD

The renowned Irish poet Brendan Kennelly was born on 17 April 1936. To mark and celebrate his 75th birthday the editors of this volume have made a new selection from his poetic oeuvre which, they believe, represents the essential Kennelly.

The poet's birthplace was the small north Kerry village of Ballylongford, where he spent the childhood that would resurface memorably in many of his poems. It is recalled in his work as the primal place of familial relationships, of a local community with its legends and lore, its gossip, stories, songs and ballads, and as a setting close to the natural world with its splendours and casual brutalities, yet open to history and the great world beyond. Kennelly took his first steps into that wider world at the local national school and then at St Ita's School in the larger Kerry town of Tarbet. There he received the education that allowed him to matriculate at Trinity College, Dublin, where he read English and French.

Upon graduation in 1961 with a first class honours degree he embarked on a doctoral thesis on the role of mythology in 19th-century Anglo-Irish verse. While working on this he spent a year in the northern English city of Leeds before returning to the Dublin where he would thereafter make his home (with sojourns in the United States and visits as poet and lecturer to many countries). He was appointed Junior Lecturer in English at Trinity in 1963, was awarded his doctoral degree in 1966 and was honoured by the university in 1973 when he was appointed to a personal chair in Modern Literature. This he occupied with distinction until his retirement in 2005.

In his poetry the Dublin in which he has spent the greater part of his adult life can seem the urban equivalent of the childhood village, an intimately known place that opens a window on the universe and on the myriad doings of his fellow men and women. Kennelly's poetry is instinctively sociable, hospitable as it is to the lives, voices, deeds and defining deaths of a host of characters.

Brendan Kennelly began publishing poetry as an undergraduate at Trinity where he took his turn as editor of *Icarus*, the literary magazine where fellow poets Derek Mahon, Michael Longley and Eavan Boland also published early work. His first full collection *Let Fall No Burning Leaf* appeared in 1963; while his most recent, *Reservoir Voices*, came out in 2009.

In a poetic career lasting more than five decades Kennelly has published countless poems in newspapers, literary magazines, periodicals; he has issued small pamphlets, slim volumes, substantial collections, selected poems and the epic-sized volumes, *Cromwell*, *The Book of Judas* and *Poetry My Arse*, which have made amplitude sometimes seem like unwieldy bulk in a body of work that will surely pose a challenge to the bibliographer. And all this has been accompanied by his forays into drama (where his versions of classical authors have won him deserved plaudits), by his two early novels, by his work as an anthologist and editor, by critical essays and reviews, and by lively journalism and social commentary.

In addition, a public persona was generated in the media that tended to obscure how the poet's life has, in fact, been intently dedicated to the practice of an art rooted in solitude and privacy: an art that he shared most fully with his public in the many readings from his work he has so generously given throughout Ireland and abroad. For some, such abundance and availability seemed the point where the prolific risked becoming the profligate, as talent can disperse itself in mere productivity and performance. The critical response to the Kennelly oeuvre has been varied, it must be admitted, as if no academic consensus can be reached on a body of work so lucidly intense, so fluently extensive and capacious (and it's in academe that poetic reputations are currently established, however one might regret that fact). This selection, by contrast, is made by its editors in the shared conviction that Brendan Kennelly is a poet of rare gifts, who at all stages of his career has written distinctive, memorable and powerful poems. We hope that this selection will allow readers to appreciate anew, or for the first time, a body of work that ranges from tender lyricism to the bleakest despair at the human condition, from bawdily comic narrative to the pleasingly epigrammatic squib, from mythic consciousness to social satire.

We have arranged the work chronologically, taking the individual poems in the order in which they were first collected in volume form (this contrasts with the poet's own predilection for publishing work thematically in selected editions, with creative disregard for such chronology). This arrangement will allow readers to gain a sense of the shape and substance of Kennelly's poetic career, while it highlights poems that are essential in his achievement.

A note of awe-struck lyricism before the wonder of being was sounded early in Kennelly's career, and has endured throughout his life as a poet. In that mood the world is vested with animistic presence so that time seems a medium which holds the reader in rapt equilibrium with the palpable given-ness of things in their absolute otherness. 'Bread', read together with such poems as 'Let It Go' and 'A Kind of Trust', epitomises those moments in Kennelly's work when consciousness enters a riskily open-ended present tense. And poems of recall such as 'The Smell' and 'The Horse's Head' so vividly resurrect childhood experiences that they enter a kind of perpetual now. Indeed, dynamic, even disorientating interactions between past and present have been an abiding preoccupation of this poet for whom time seems to constitute a force-field of imaginative relationships, a zone which the living and the dead inhabit as images of themselves (this in part accounts for the atemporal way in which Kennelly has arranged his selected editions).

Such a plastic sense of time makes of Kennelly's oeuvre a poetic theatre of dreams, and of nightmares, with history, as well as immediate personal experience and recollection, supplying the *dramatis personae*. It was *Cromwell* (published in 1983) that brought this aspect of his work to full realisation. The horrors and atrocities confronted in that volume exposed how the lyrical strain sounded in the early work had not not been free of discordancies. Outright terror, for example, could disturb the lyrical tenderness of an early love poem such as 'Dream of a Black Fox', but notes of disgust, fierce satire and sardonic bitterness made *Cromwell* almost unremittingly a work of dissonant energy. The poet's obsession with selfhood in thrall to otherness finds dramatic expression in a poetic sequence (with the sonnet as a normative form cooling in a grimly controlled way the fevered phantasmagoria of the work's inspiration) that sets in black-comic apposition a figure of the quintessential Irishman and a composite version of the Lord Protector, compact of a terrifying rhetoric, dark deeds and cartoonish absurdity. Time, in a sequence where everything happens simultaneously, with anachronism a condition of a grotesque normality, readily segues into mythic dimensions. Here psychological forces that affect the construction of selfhood and determine the course of history, vie for mastery.

The predominately psychological focus of *Cromwell* was intensified in Kennelly's voluminous work of 1991, *The Book of Judas: A Poem*. Where *Cromwell* reckons selfhood an arena in which identity was fissile, fundamentally unstable, this self-lacerating work makes the heart of man a site of endless treachery. Through the persona of a derided and eternally-damned Judas (a figure variously derived in the compulsive inventiveness of the book, from scripture, art, legend, folklore, the argot of the street), self-betrayal is seen to define the human condition. It is Kennelly's dark night of the soul, where blasphemy is courted as paradoxical testament to all that betrayal betrays. Its bleak vision of modernity is redeemed from simplistic nihilism, none-theless, by the force of its excoriating satire, and by a religious impulse that makes Judas the crux of an existential anguish.

Language in *The Book of Judas* is seen as an instrument of betrayal, along with money, sexuality, political power, the media. In *Poetry My Arse* (1995) Kennelly rounded on his own art, poetry itself, as perhaps the most treacherous of the things that make deception ubiquitous. On one level the work lampoons prevailing cultural values whereby in an Ireland of rampant commercialism poetry is afforded pious veneration as a spiritual asset that somehow stands to the nation's credit, when the main business of life is crass material enrichment. In the book's occasionally heavy-handed comedy the poet Ace de Horner (a verbal play on *Aosdána*, the Irish state's academy of the arts) with his dog Kanooce (playing on *Cnuas*, the allowance paid to some members by *Aosdána*) by strategems and ruses opportun-istically negotiates a Dublin degraded by a febrile, always energetic vulgarity. That the poetry racket pays in its own demeaning way, is one disillusioned message of the volume's comic brio.

However, the book's disillusionment, with its poet going blind, is also of a deeper kind. It implies that, in exploiting experience as its subject-matter, poetry is in fact being true to its own treacherously predatory nature. A tone of sustained mockery, dead-pan and invincibly unimpressed, is, therefore, a stringently liberating, if discomfiting register in this work, that sets in question the very lyricism that has defined Kennelly himself on other notable poetic occasions. Yet each literary mode – the lyrical and its obverse, a reductively satiric assault on 'the poetic' – shares what has seemed the basis of all of Kennelly's poetry: a quest for authenticity of emotion undertaken with high moral intent. In each, as Beckett said of the painter Jack Yeats, the poet 'stakes his being'.

Not that, in the three major works that absorbed Kennelly between about 1980 and 1995, the lyrical is entirely occluded. For even as the poet immerses himself in the destructive elements of the Cromwellian subjection of Ireland, in a pained study of the nature and pervasiveness of betrayal and admits radical doubt about poetry's very validity, lyric feeling keeps breaking through. It is as if the lonely, generous vulnerabilty, to which it bears witness, is ineradicable in his sensibility. Indeed where these works are invaded by lyrical feeling, that feeling, in the challenging contexts in which it emerges, acquires a haunting, authenticating rigour, all its own.

These three major works also possess an air of a poet seeking to impose (perhaps not always successfully) a different kind of rigour on what can seem self-generating, burgeoning texts. For they are marked by an increasing tendency towards the formally exacting, the aphoristic and the epigramatic. Where in *Cromwell* sonnets (dubbed 'genetic epics' in the poem) seek to give manageable shape to a nightmarish burden of history, in *The Book of Judas* and *Poetry My Arse* individual poems frequently move towards a clinching summation: comic, desolate, absurd by turns. An impression mounts of the highflown and rhetorical insistently nailed to the deck of reality, as it were, pinned down by the conclusive apothegm. The effect is tonic.

This taste for the epigram means that in the Latin poet Martial Kennelly, so concerned throughout his career to give a voice to radical otherness, finds a true brother in spirit. The impact of Martial during the last decade is not only evident in Kennelly's lively versions published as *Martial Art* in 2003, but also in his more recent attempts to compress lyric or satiric observation in the span of a few telling lines (*Now* published in 2006 is a book of three-liners). Where once reigned an embarrassment of riches, a zest for poetic economy has brought its own valuable rewards to this poet of abundant gifts.

TERENCE BROWN
& MICHAEL LONGLEY
Dublin – Belfast
January 2011

BIBLIOGRAPHICAL NOTE & ACKNOWLEDGEMENTS

The poems in *The Essential Brendan Kennelly* are taken more or less chronologically from the following collections:

Let Fall No Burning Leaf (Dublin: New Square Publications, 1963)

Collection One: Getting Up Early (Dublin: Allen Figgis, 1966)

Dream of a Black Fox (Dublin: Allen Figgis, 1968)

Bread (Dublin: Tara Telephone Publications, 1971)

Love Cry (Dublin: Allen Figgis, 1972)

Salvation the Stranger (Dublin: Tara Telephone Publications, 1972)

A Kind of Trust (Dublin: Gallery Books, 1975)

New and Selected Poems (Dublin: Gallery Books, 1976)

The Visitor (Dublin: St Bueno's Press, 1978)

In Spite of the Wise (Dublin: Trinity Closet Press, 1979)

The Boats Are Home (Dublin: Gallery Books, 1980)

The House That Jack Didn't Build (Dublin: Beaver Row Press, 1982)

Cromwell: A Poem (Dublin: Beaver Row Press, 1983; corrected edition, Newcastle upon Tyne: Bloodaxe Books, 1987)

Selected Poems (Dublin: Kerrymount Publications, 1985)

Love of Ireland: Poems from the Irish (Cork & Dublin: Mercier Press, 1989)

A Time for Voices: Selected Poems 1960-1990 (Newcastle upon Tyne: Bloodaxe Books, 1990)

The Book of Judas: A Poem (Newcastle upon Tyne: Bloodaxe Books, 1991); abridged edition, *The Little Book of Judas* (Tarset: Bloodaxe Books, 2002)

Breathing Spaces: Early Poems (Newcastle upon Tyne: Bloodaxe Books, 1992)

Poetry My Arse: A Poem (Newcastle upon Tyne: Bloodaxe Books, 1995)

The Man Made of Rain (Newcastle upon Tyne: Bloodaxe Books, 1998)

Begin (Newcastle upon Tyne: Bloodaxe Books, 1999)

Glimpses (Tarset: Bloodaxe Books, 2001)

Martial Art (Tarset: Bloodaxe Books, 2003)

Familiar Strangers: New & Selected Poems 1960-2004 (Tarset: Bloodaxe Books, 2004)

Now (Tarset: Bloodaxe Books, 2006)

Reservoir Voices (Tarset: Bloodaxe Books, 2009)

Except in the case of collections that are also sequences, individual collections are not named in the contents listing. Most poems from collections published up until 1990 are reprinted from *Familiar Strangers*, which is still in print and includes all of *The Man Made of Rain*.

THE ESSENTIAL BRENDAN KENNELLY

Adam

Two loves were quite enough, herself and God,
(God knows how hard it was to have to choose!)
Green shoots of innocence sprang from the sod,
Wild tendrils whispered that he couldn't lose.
High disobedience roared through his blood,
His heart beat faster, suddenly stood still,
He found another way beyond the good
And little doubts, like puddles, stained his will.
A graceful world snapped, an axis jarred,
Long, shabby fields appeared, the sunlight thinned
In places under skies become ill-starred
Through rage of storm and ice and cold and wind
He, darkly conscious, touched her darkened will,
Grew grim, suspicious, furtive; loved her still.

The Gift

It came slowly.
Afraid of insufficient self-content
Or some inherent weakness in itself
Small and hesitant
Like children at the tops of stairs
It came through shops, rooms, temples,
Streets, places that were badly-lit.
It was a gift that took me unawares
And I accepted it.

Westland Row

Brown bag bulging with fading nothings;
A ticket for three pounds one and six
To Euston, London via Holyhead:
Young faces limp, misunderstanding
What the first gay promptings meant –
A pass into a brilliant wilderness,
A Capital of hopeless promise.
Well, mount the steps: lug the bag:
Take your place. And out of all the crowd,
Watch the girl in the wrinkled coat,
    Her face half-grey.
    Her first time.

Before Leaving...

Before leaving, say something; speak of the long, wet
Fingers of rain that probed the whiteness of your face,
As you walked, head into the frail February light,
Beyond the heaving city's distant rim.
Say a word or two; tell why you set
Your step in muted strength to walk a place
Where silence sprawled across a dim
Line of houses, leaning against the night.
A word about the sand that crept
Against the grasses in the summer haze;
About the time that trickled by
Unnoticed into angry winter days;
About the flooding life that swept
The anger Aprilwards to die.
Say something then, before
Leaving. A word or two. No more.

Moloney Up and At It

My soul from hell, the night the ould wan died,
Moloney said, I cried an' cried
Tears down. I'd been tied to her string
Through rack and hardship and the wild fling
O' youth, through manhood and the grey
Days when youth begins to slip away,
And now my addled heart and head
Were bound by the memory of the dead.

    Well, anyway, after puttin' herself down
In the box, I went to the town
O' Lishtowel for a few drinks, and there
I met a Knockanore woman with red hair
And gamey eye. I made bold
And in a short time had told
Her my story. She cocked her ear and listened well.
We drank until the darkness fell
And for hours after. The talk
Spun on love. 'Can I walk
A piece with you?' says I. 'Moloney,' says she,
'You're welcome to do what you like with me.'
Fair enough! We left Lishtowel and struck the road,
Footin' it free over pothole
And gravel. The Knockanore woman was full o' guff
And harped on all the tricks o' love.
I upped with my question. She
Was willin' and free.
'Where would you like it?' says I. 'Well,' she said,
'God's green earth is a warm bed.'
'Right you are, girl,' says I.
It happened we were passin' by
Gale graveyard where my mother lay.
'What would you say
To this place?' says I. 'Moloney,' says she,
'If it's right with you, it's right with me.'

Straightaway, I opened the gate and led
The Knockanore woman over the dead
O' seven parishes. Talk of a flyer!
Fasht as they come an' hot as fire!
She fell down on the soft clay
Of a fresh grave, and before I could say
A word, I was on the ground as well,
Goin' like the hammers o' hell!
'Twas only then I saw where I was.
On my mother's grave! But that was no cause
For panic, though I was a bit
Upset at first by the strangeness of it.
The Knockanore woman was happy as Larry,
And I was sparkin' and merry
As a cricket. 'Yerra, you might
As well enjoy the gift o' the night
While you have the chance,' I said
To myself, realisin' the dead are dead,
Past holiness and harms –
And the livin' woman was in my arms.

    'Twas great fun
While it lasted, and it lasted long. The sun
Was startin' to climb the sky when we rose
Up and settled our clothes.
'How are you, girl?' says I.
'Yerra, fine,' says she.
''Twas a fine night,' says I.
''Twas so, but a bit cold towards mornin',' says she,
'And I wouldn't mind a hot cup o' tay
This minute.' 'You're a wise woman,' I said,
'Let them say whatever they say,
There's wan thing sure. 'Tis hard to bate the cup o' tay.'
And then, 'Whisht,' I said,
Suddenly remembering the quiet dead.
With the memory, I started to sing,
Then and there, a bar of a jig,
And as I sang I danced as well
On the body whose soul was in heaven or hell.

'You're a gay man,' says she, 'to bring
Me to a place like this for your bit of a fling,
And I'm thinkin' the love has gone to your head
When you dance a jig on the bones o' the dead.'
Said I, 'By the Christ that is divine,
If I have a son may he dance on mine.
While a man has the chance he should dance and sing,' I said,
'For he'll be the hell of a long time dead.
So come on now without further ado
And I'll put on the kettle for the tay.'
She smiled and we started on our way
In the early light that was breakin' for day.

The night was lost, the daylight stretched ahead,
Behind me slept the unforgettable dead,
Beside me stepped a woman with gamey eye,
Laughin' as the sun mounted the sky.

My Dark Fathers

My dark fathers lived the intolerable day
Committed always to the night of wrong,
Stiffened at the hearthstone, the woman lay,
Perished feet nailed to her man's breastbone.
Grim houses beckoned in the swelling gloom
Of Munster fields where the Atlantic night
Fettered the child within the pit of doom,
And everywhere a going down of light.

And yet upon the sandy Kerry shore
The woman once had danced at ebbing tide
Because she loved flute music – and still more
Because a lady wondered at the pride
Of one so humble. That was long before
The green plant withered by an evil chance;
When winds of hunger howled at every door
She heard the music dwindle and forgot the dance.

Such mercy as the wolf receives was hers
Whose dance became a rhythm in a grave,
Achieved beneath the thorny savage furze
That yellowed fiercely in a mountain cave.
Immune to pity, she, whose crime was love,
Crouched, shivered, searched the threatening sky,
Discovered ready signs, compelled to move
Her to her innocent appalling cry.

Skeletoned in darkness, my dark fathers lay
Unknown, and could not understand
The giant grief that trampled night and day,
The awful absence moping through the land.
Upon the headland, the encroaching sea
Left sand that hardened after tides of Spring,
No dancing feet disturbed its symmetry
And those who loved good music ceased to sing.

Since every moment of the clock
Accumulates to form a final name,
Since I am come of Kerry clay and rock,
I celebrate the darkness and the shame
That could compel a man to turn his face
Against the wall, withdrawn from light so strong
And undeceiving, spancelled in a place
Of unapplauding hands and broken song.

Getting Up Early

Getting up early promises well;
    a milkhorse on the road
induces thoughts of a sleeping world
    and a waking God.

This hour has something sacred;
    bells will be ringing soon,
but now I am content to watch
    the day begin to bloom.

I would only waste my breath
    on poor superfluous words;
how perfectly they wing for me –
    the new invisible birds

who celebrate the light that spreads
    like love to window sills
as morning steps like a laughing girl
    down from the Dublin hills.

Lislaughtin Abbey

Flashing starlings twist and turn
    in the sky above my head,
while in Lislaughtin Abbey lie
    the packed anticipating dead.

Silent generations there
    that long had bent the knee
endow the Shannon with the grace
    of reaching to the sea.

Swollen by the rich juice of the dead
    the Shannon moves with ease
towards a mighty union with
    Atlantic mysteries.

But though the river sweeps beyond
    each congested bone,
its currents do not swirl towards
    a resurrection,

any more than starlings do
    that, fearing death this winter day,
create small thunder in the sky
    and shelter where they may,

ignoring green Lislaughtin where
    subtle shadows pass
through shattered altars, broken walls,
    the blood of martyrs in the grass,

into the ground that winters well
    and blossoms soon or late,
preserving patient multitudes
    who are content to wait

till they at last disturb the stones,
    the fox's lair, the starling's nest,
to cry out with the howling damned,
    to wonder with the Blessed,

to hear the word for which they wait
    under the coarse grass
the meanest blade of which assists
    in what must come to pass,

to see why silent centuries
    have finally sufficed
to purge all in the rising flood
    of the overflowing blood of Christ.

Restless at the gate, I turn away
    groping towards what can't be said
and I know I know but little
    of the birds, the river and the dead.

God's Eye

Beneath the stare of God's gold burning eye,
Two crisp hands clap; a thousand plover rise
And wheel across the clean meadows of the sky.

Black wings flash and gleam; a perfect white
Makes beautiful each rising breast,
Sovereign in the far-off miracle of flight
Swollen by the rich juice of the dead

Their terror is a lovely thing,
A sudden inspiration, exploding
In the thunder of each beating wing;

A startling rout, as of an army driven
In broken regiments
Against the proud, fantastic face of heaven.

And yet, no mad disorder, no raucous accident
Deforms the miracle; high flocks
Fulfil an inbred, furious intent.

In screams of dread, perfection whirls
Along the headlands of the sky;
They circle, gabbing now like girls,

And wing to safety in Carrig Wood,
Dip through branches, disappear; across the sky,
The pale sun throws a quilt of solitude.

After terror, they are safety's prisoners,
Momentary victims of security
In labyrinths where surly winter stirs.

They breathe on branches, hidden and alone.
Fear will flare again, but now the abandoned sky
Is turning cold and grey as stone.

I think about that marvellous rout, the empty sky,
A flight of plover hidden from
The stare of God's gold burning eye.

Begin

Begin again to the summoning birds
to the sight of light at the window,
begin to the roar of morning traffic
all along Pembroke Road.
Every beginning is a promise
born in light and dying in dark
determination and exaltation of springtime
flowering the way to work.
Begin to the pageant of queuing girls
the arrogant loneliness of swans in the canal
bridges linking the past and future
old friends passing though with us still.
Begin to the loneliness that cannot end
since it perhaps is what makes us begin,
begin to wonder at unknown faces
at crying birds in the sudden rain
at branches stark in the willing sunlight
at seagulls foraging for bread
at couples sharing a sunny secret
alone together while making good.
Though we live in a world that dreams of ending
that always seems about to give in
something that will not acknowledge conclusion
insists that we forever begin.

The Pig-killer

On the scoured table, the pig lies
On its back, its legs held down
By Ned Gorman and Joe Dineen.
Over its throat, knife in hand, towers

Fitzmaurice, coatless, his face and hands
Brown as wet hay. He has travelled
Seven miles for this kill and now,
Eager to do a good job, examines

The prone bulk. Tenderly his fingers move
On the flabby neck, seeking the right spot
For the knife. Finding it, he leans
Nearer and nearer the waiting throat,

Expert fingers fondling flesh. Nodding then
To Gorman and Dineen, he raises the knife,
Begins to trace a line along the throat.
Slowly the line turns red, the first sign

Of blood appears, spreads shyly over the skin. The pig
Begins to scream. Fitzmaurice halts his blade
In the middle of the red line, lifts it slightly,
Plunges it eight inches deep

Into the pig. In a flash, the brown hands
Are red, and the pig's screams
Rise and fall with the leaping blood. The great heaving
Body relaxes for Gorman and Dineen.

Fitzmaurice stands back, lays his knife on
A window-sill, asks for hot water and soap.
Blade and hands he vigorously purges, then
Slipping on his battered coat,

Eyeing the pig, says with authority –
'Dead as a doornail! Still as a mouse!
There's a good winter's feedin' in that baishte!'
Fitzmaurice turns and strides into the house.

Death of a Strong Man

That night, as always, he spoke of cattle,
The pint glass snug in his great fist,
A man whose name for strength had travelled
From his own parish to the tip o' Dingle.
On the way home, he was cut down,
His massive promise become sudden loss,
It took him four days to die and then
His friends put up a commemorative cross.
Now, in the city, seeing grim
Headlights tigering through night,
Luminous eyes that flash
In midnight dark, I think of him
Who left the pub's comfortable light
To be broken and remembered on the roadside grass.

Dream of a Black Fox

The black fox loped out of the hills
And circled for several hours,
Eyes bright with menace, teeth
White in the light, tail dragging the ground.
The woman in my arms cringed with fear,
Collapsed crying, her head hurting my neck.
She became dumb fear.

The black fox, big as a pony,
Circled and circled,
Whimsical executioner,
Torment dripping like saliva from its jaws.
Too afraid to show my fear,
I watched it as it circled;
Then it leaped across me
Its great black body breaking the air,
Landing on a wall above my head.

Turning then, it looked at me.

And I saw it was magnificent,
Ruling the darkness, lord of its element,
Scorning all who are afraid,
Seeming even to smile
At human pettiness and fear.

The woman in my arms looked up
At this lord of darkness
And as quickly hid her head again.
Then the fox turned and was gone
Leaving us with fear
And safety –
Every usual illusion.

Quiet now, no longer trembling,
She lay in my arms,
Still as a sleeping child.

I knew I had seen fear,
Fear dispelled by what makes fear
A part of pure creation.
It might have taught me
Mastery of myself,
Dominion over death,
But was content to leap
With ease and majesty
Across the valleys and the hills of sleep.

Bread

Someone else cut off my head
In a golden field.
Now I am re-created

By her fingers. This
Moulding is more delicate
Than a first kiss,

More deliberate than her own
Rising up
And lying down,

I am fine
As anything in
This legendary garden

Yet I am nothing till
She runs her fingers through me
And shapes me with her skill.

The form that I shall bear
Grows round and white.
It seems I comfort her

Even as she slits my face
And stabs my chest.
Her feeling for perfection is

Absolute.
So I am glad to go through fire
And come out

Shaped like her dream.
In my way
I am all that can happen to men.
I came to life at her finger-ends.
I will go back into her again.

'Dear Autumn Girl'

(FROM *Love Cry*)

Dear Autumn girl, these helter-skelter days
When mad leaf-argosies drive at my head,
I try but fail to give you proper praise
For the excitement you've created
In my world: an islander at sea,
A girl with child, a fool, a simple king,
Garrulous masters of true mockery –
My hugest world becomes the littlest thing

Whenever you walk smiling though a room
And your flung golden hair is still wet
Ready for September's homaged rays;
I see what is, I wonder what's to come,
I bless what you remember or forget
And recognise the poverty of praise.

A Giving

Here in this room, this December day,
Listening to the year die on the warfields
And in the voices of children
Who laugh in the indecisive light
At the throes that but rehearse their own
I take the mystery of giving in my hands
And pass it on to you.

I give thanks
To the giver of images,
The reticent god who goes about his work
Determined to hold on to nothing.
Embarrassed at the prospect of possession
He distributes leaves to the wind
And lets them pitch and leap like boys
Capering out of their skin.
Pictures are thrown behind hedges,
Poems skitter backwards over cliffs,
There is a loaf of bread on Derek's threshold
And we will never know who put it there.

For such things
And bearing in mind
The midnight hurt, the shot bride,
The famine in the heart,
The demented soldier, the terrified cities
Rising out of their own rubble,

I give thanks.

I listen to the sound of doors
Opening and closing in the street.
They are like the heartbeats of this creator
Who gives everything away.
I do not understand
Such constant evacuation of the heart,
Such striving towards emptiness.

Thinking, however, of the intrepid skeleton,
The feared definition,
I grasp a little of the giving
And hold it close as my own flesh.

It is this little
That I give to you.
And now I want to walk out and witness
The shadow of some ungraspable sweetness
Passing over the measureless squalor of man
Like a child's hand over my own face
Or the exodus of swallows across the land

And I know it does not matter
That I do not understand.

Birth

I don't know if I shall be
Speaking or silent, laughing or crying,
When it comes to me

Out of this distant place
To shine at the window, rustle the curtains,
Brush my face

More lightly than gossamer,
So inspiring and fragile
I shall not dare to stir

Or hardly breathe until I sense
In my heart and mind
Its delicate omnipotence.

I may know then
The price and value of stillness
Commonly ignored by men

And be content to feel
It possess me,
Steal

Through my remotest countries
And establish its rule
Where, my bravest days,

I would not dare to venture.
Then, if I find courage enough,
I may speak in a manner

Befitting this thing.
God help me the moment
My heart starts opening

To comprehend and give.
I will be born in that hour of grace.
I will begin to live.

Let It Go

Let it go
Out of reach, out of sight,
Out of the door and the window,

Through the city,
Over the mountains
And the sea.

I do not mean a mere escape,
A deliberate loosening
Of a brutal grip

Like that of church on soul,
Father on son
Or even love on the lover's beautiful

Surrender to the dear pain,
Or any sin or sickness that could
Swallow a man.

I mean a different thing
Beyond desire to acquire or captivate,
A felt relinquishing

Such as can be seen
When the air yields to the bird
Or the green

Trunk of a tree surrenders
To the tactful advance of moss
Or when the river stirs

Its surface
To accept a drifting stick.
I feel such courtesy

When I let it go
From me to countries
I will never know

And I stand, hoping to discern
Its breath in my heart
At its return.

A Kind of Trust

I am happy now.
You rose from your sick bed
After three weeks. Your heart was low

When the world grew small,
A white ceiling
And four yellow walls.

Let me say again what this means
To me. As far as I know
Love always begins

Like a white morning
Of seagulls near the window,
Messengers bringing

Word that we must up and out
Into a small garden
Where there are late

Apples we shall find
So ripe that the slightest touch
Will pitch them to the ground.

Best things seem content to fall and fail.
I am not good enough for that.
I fight the drag and pull

Of any kind of dying
And bitterly insist
On that white morning

When you weakly climb the stairs,
Letting new life reach you like a gift
There at the brown banister.

I do not insist
Out of panic or vague dread
But out of a kind of trust

In this beginning
With late apples and early seagulls
And a young sun shining

When you let cold water flow into a cup,
Steady yourself between two chairs
And stand straight up.

The Kiss

'Go down to the room and kiss him,
There's not much left o' him in the bed.
He had a good run of it, over eighty years.
In a few days he'll be dead.'

My nine years shook at the words 'kiss him'.
I knew the old man was something to my father.
I knew I had to do what my father said.
I trembled to the bedroom door

And entered the room where the drawn curtains
Foiled the light.
Jack Boland was a white wreck on the pillows,
His body a slight

Hump under the eiderdown quilt, starred white and red,
Everything under the black crucifix
With gaping mouth and bleeding head.
He saw me, half-lifted a hand. 'Here, boy,' he said.

I walked across the bedroom floor
And felt the ice in his hands enter mine.
His eyes were screwed up with sickness, his hair was wet,
His tongue hung, slapped back. Every bone

In my body chilled as I bent my head
To the smell and feel of the sickspittle on his lips.
I kissed him, I find it hard to say what I kissed
But I drank him into me when I kissed him.

I recognised something of what in him was ending,
Of what in me had scarcely begun.
He seemed without fear, I think I gave him nothing,
He told me something of what it is to be alone.

There is no way to say goodbye to the dying.
Jack Boland said 'G'wan, boy! Go now.'
I shivered away from his hands, his smell,
The wet blobs of pain on hair and brow,

The weak, eager touch. My childfear
Went with me out into the corridor, stayed
Inside me till I stood again at my father's side,
Head down, thinking I was no longer afraid

Yet feeling still the deathlips rummaging at my lips,
The breath a sick warmth mingling with my breath.
It's thirty years since I bent my head to the kiss.
Ten thirties would not make me forget.

The Visitor

He strutted into the house.

Laughing
He walked over to the woman
Stuck a kiss in her face.

He wore gloves.
He had fur on his coat.
He was the most confident man in the world.
He liked his own wit.

Turning his attention to the children
He patted each one on the head.
They are healthy but a bit shy, he said.
They'll make fine men and women, he said.

The children looked up at him.
He was still laughing.
He was so confident
They could not find the word for it.
He was so elegant
He was more terrifying than the giants of night.

The world
Could only go on its knees before him.
The kissed woman
Was expected to adore him.

It seemed she did.

I'll eat now, he said,
Nothing elaborate, just something simple and quick –
Rashers, eggs, sausages, tomatoes
And a few nice lightly-buttered slices
Of your very own
Home-made brown
Bread.

O you dear woman, can't you see
My tongue is hanging out
For a pot of your delicious tea.
No other woman in this world
Can cook so well for me.

I'm always touched by your modest mastery!

He sat at table like a king.
He ate between bursts of laughter.
He was a great philosopher,
Wise, able to advise,
Solving the world between mouthfuls.
The woman hovered about him.
The children stared at his vital head.
He had robbed them of every word they had.
Please have some more food, the woman said.
He ate, he laughed, he joked,
He knew the world, his plate was clean
As Jack Spratt's in the funny poem,
He was a handsome wolfman,
More gifted than anyone
The woman and children of that house
Had ever seen or known.

He was the storm they listened to at night
Huddled together in bed
He was what laid the woman low
With the killing pain in her head
He was the threat in the high tide
At the back of the house
He was a huge knock on the door
In a moment of peace
He was a hound's neck leaning
Into the kill
He was a hawk of heaven stooping
To fulfil its will
He was the sentence tired writers of gospel
Prayed God to write

He was a black explosion of starlings
Out of a November tree
He was a plan that worked
In a climate of self-delight
He was all the voices
Of the sea.

My time is up, he said,
I must go now.

Taking his coat, gloves, philosophy, laughter, wit,
He prepared to leave.
He kissed the woman again.
He smiled down on the children.
He walked out of the house.
The children looked at each other.
The woman looked at the chair.
The chair was a throne
Bereft of its king, its visitor.

Poem from a Three Year Old

And will the flowers die?

And will the people die?

And every day do you grow old, do I
grow old, no I'm not old, do
flowers grow old?

Old things – do you throw them out?

Do you throw old people out?

And how you know a flower that's old?

The petals fall, the petals fall from flowers,
and do the petals fall from people too,
every day more petals fall until the
floor where I would like to play I
want to play is covered with old
flowers and people all the same
together lying there with petals fallen
on the dirty floor I want to play
the floor you come and sweep
with the huge broom.

The dirt you sweep, what happens that,
what happens all the dirt you sweep
from flowers and people, what
happens all the dirt? Is all the
dirt what's left of flowers and
people, all the dirt there in a
heap under the huge broom that
sweeps everything away?

Why you work so hard, why brush
and sweep to make a heap of dirt?
And who will bring new flowers?

And who will bring new people? Who will
bring new flowers to put in water
where no petals fall on to the
floor where I would like to
play? Who will bring new flowers
that will not hang their heads
like tired old people wanting sleep?
Who will bring new flowers that
do not split and shrivel every
day? And if we have new flowers,
will we have new people too to
keep the flowers alive and give
them water?

And will the new young flowers die?

And will the new young people die?

And why?

The Singing Girl Is Easy in Her Skill

The singing girl is easy in her skill.
We are more human than we were before.
We cannot see just now why men should kill

Although it seems we are condemned to spill
The blood responding to the ocean's roar.
The singing girl is easy in her skill.

That light transfiguring the window-sill
Is peace that shyly knocks on every door.
We cannot see just now why men should kill.

This room, this house, this world all seem to fill
With faith in which no human heart is poor.
The singing girl is easy in her skill.

Though days are maimed by many a murderous will
And lovers shudder at what lies in store
We cannot see just now why men should kill.

It's possible we may be happy still,
No living heart can ever ask for more.
We cannot see just now why men should kill.
The singing girl is easy in her skill.

Living Ghosts

Richard Broderick celebrates
This winter's first and only fall of snow
With a midnight rendering
of *The Bonny Bunch of Roses O*

And Paddy Dineen is rising
With *On Top of the Old Stone Wall.*
His closed eyes respect the song.
His mind's a festival.

And now *Romona* lights the lips
Of swaying Davy Shea.
In a world of possibilities
This is the only way.

His face a summer morning
When the sun decides to smile
Tom Keane touches enchantment
With *Charming Carrig Isle.*

I've seen men in their innocence
Untroubled by right and wrong.
I close my eyes and see them
Becoming song.

All the songs are living ghosts
And long for a living voice.
O may another fall of snow
Bid Broderick rejoice!

To Learn

There were nine fields between him and the school.
The first field was deep like his father's frown
The second was a nervous pony
The third a thistle with a purple crown
The fourth was a suspicious glance
The fifth rambled like a drinker's talk
The sixth was all wet treachery
The seventh was a man who did too much work
The eighth was downcast eyes, determined to be tame,
The ninth said hello, goodbye.
He thought of the nine fields in turn
As he beat the last ditch and came
In sight of the school on the gravelly rise.
He buckled down to learn.

The Smell

The inside of the church absorbed the rain's thunder,
Lightning deceived and killed, the thunder never lied,
The thunder knelt and prayed at the high altar.
I was six years old. I knelt and prayed at her side.

She was a woman in black, she of the white head,
She whose lips rivalled the lips of the rain.
Someone closer to her than anyone had died far back.
That was the story. The story created her pain.

Out of her pain she prayed, always on her knees,
Her lips shaped secrets like rain in August grass.
Her white head, I knew, could not betray or deceive,
The thunder imitated the secrets of her heart.

I knelt at her side, my shoulder brushing her black,
Her lips surrendered visions of her private heaven and hell.
Drugged by her whispers, my head sank into her side,
My body and soul, in that instant, entered her smell,

Not merely the smell of her skin, but the smell
Of her prayers and pain, the smell of her long loss,
The smell of the years that had whitened her head,
That made her whisper to the pallid Christ on his cross,

The rent, dumb Christ, listener at the doors of the heart,
The pummelled Christ, the sea of human pain,
The sated Christ, the drinker of horrors,
The prisoner Christ, dungeoned in flesh and bone.

Her smell opened her locked world,
My closed eyes saw something of mine,
My small world swam in her infinite world
And did not drown but rose where the sun shone

On silence following the thunder's majestic prayer
For all the pain of all the living and dead,
I opened my eyes to the silence
Blessing her black clothes, her white head,

Blessing the smell that had told me something
Beyond lips' whispers and heart's prayer.
She took my hand in her hand, we moved together
Out of the church into the rain-cleaned air.

The Horse's Head

'Hold the horse's head,' the farmer said
To the boy loitering outside the pub.
'If you're willing to hold the horse's head
You'll earn a shilling.'

The boy took the reins, the farmer went inside,
The boy stood near the horse's head.

The horse's head was above the boy's head.
The boy looked up.
The sun attended the horse's head, a crown of light
Blinded the boy's eyes for a moment.

His eyes cleared and he saw the horse's head,
Eyes, ears, mane, wet
Nostrils, brown forehead splashed white,
Nervous lips,
Teeth moving on the bit.

The sun fussed over it.
The boy stared at it.
He reached up and gave the horse's head
A pat.

The horse's head shuddered, pulled on the reins,
Rasping the boy's hands, almost burning the skin,
Drawing blood to attention.
The boy's grip tightened on the reins,
Jerked the horse's head to order.
The boy was not afraid.
He would be master of the horse's head
Made of the sun
In the street outside the pub
Where the farmer stood drinking at the bar.

Daylight said the boy was praying
His head bowed before an altar.
The air itself became the prayer
Unsaid
Shared between the boy
And the horse's head.

The horse's head guarded the boy
Looking down from its great height.
If the boy should stumble
The horse's head would bear him up,
Raise him, as before,
To his human stature.

If he should lay his head against the horse's head –
Peace.

The farmer came out of the pub.
He gave the boy a shilling.
He led the horse away.
The boy stared at the horse.
He felt the reins in his hands
Now easy, now rasping,
And over his head, forever,
The horse's head
Between the earth and the sun.
He put the shilling in his pocket
And walked on.

The Names of the Dead Are Lightning

'All my old friends are dying,'
You say in your letter,
Last night the wind cried

Through the house and the rain
Flailed at the streets and trees.
I thought of your loss

Knowing too well,
If I tried for weeks,
Not a syllable

Would salve your wound.
Tice. Joe. Jackie. Gone.
Father, why does the sound

Of thunder make me seek
The darkest room in the house,
Sit and wait for the blue flick

Of lightning over the walls?
You know how I hate loud voices
But this voice called

As though it would not be denied
From heaven to earth, from earth
To heaven. All night I tried

To decipher its tone of cosmic command
But all I found was your letter
Flickering in my mind

The darkest place I know.
The names of the dead are lightning.
Tice. Jackie. Joe.

The Bell

At six o'clock on a summer evening
    Danny Mulvihill rang the bell.
It could be heard out in Lislaughtin
    And down in Carrigafoyle.

The fields heard it and were still
    As Michael Enright's mind
Lulled by a field of wheat
    Goldening the ground.

Under the bridge the river calmed
    Its lifeblood towards the sea;
Touched by the bell the river kept
    Its depth for company.

At the height of the bridge Jack Jones stood alone
    Hearing the two sounds,
Through his blood flowed river and bell
    As through the summer land.

Then beyond the river adventured the bell,
    Beyond the silent man,
It lingered over every weed,
    It entered every stone,

It celebrated its own life,
    Its sense of itself as a friend
To even the midges and the briars,
    It praised its own end

Which, when it came, was hard to tell
    Since there remained on the air
Presences like happy ghosts
    Summoned from near and far.

Points of View

A neighbour said De Valéra was
As straight as Christ,
As spiritually strong.
The man in the next house said
'Twas a great pity
He wasn't crucified as young.

Calling the Shots

He was half a mile from the road, in the fields,
When they shot him from a moving truck.
He fell like a collapsing scarecrow.
They didn't bother to stop
But took the first turn
Right and pressed on,
Having a village to burn.
The grass accommodated a dead man.
He lay there
Long enough to leave his shape in the grass
Like a resting hare.

I got the loan of a rifle from Danny King
Who loved wild geese.
I knelt by a paling-post and barbed wire
And fired at a seagull in the mud.
He fell like a doll knocked from a mantelpiece.
The incoming tide lifted a wing like paper
Shuffled by the wind.

I never met the man in the fields.
I hear he was clearing scutch,
I wonder if the soldier laughed or shuddered
Or simply forgot. Was he practising
His art? Did anyone congratulate
Him on being so accurate
From such a difficult position?
I won't forget
The seagull's wing lifting in the lazy tide
Like a hand in blessing
Moments after the shot.

from **CROMWELL** (1983)

Measures

It was just that like certain of my friends I, Buffún, could not endure the emptiness. They took the measures open to them. I invited the butcher into my room and began a dialogue with him, suspecting that he'd follow a strict path of self-justification. Imagine my surprise when, with an honesty unknown to myself (for which God be thanked officially here and now) he spoke of gutted women and ashen cities, hangings and lootings, screaming soldiers and the stratagems of corrupt politicians with a cool sadness, a fluent inevitable pity. But I wasn't going to let that fool me. So, from a mountain of indignant legends, bizarre history, demented rumours and obscene folklore, I accused the butcher not merely of following the most atrocious of humanity's examples (someone was sneezing and shouting 'Mary' outside my room) but also of creating precedents of such immeasurable vileness that his name, when uttered on the lips of the unborn a thousand years hence, would ignite a rage of hate in the hearts of even the most tolerant and gentle. Imagine, I said, to create, deliberately, a name like that for yourself, to toil with such devotion towards your own immortal shame, to elect to be the very source of a tradition of loathing, the butt of jibing, despising millions. (I was really riding the old rhetoric now.)

The butcher calmly replied that the despising millions were simply millions; he was one. One. Yes, I agreed, one who makes Herod look like a benevolent Ballsbridge dad frolicking with his offspring in Herbert Park. I would remind you, returned the butcher, that you invited me here. I am the guest of your imagination, therefore have the grace to hear me out; I am not altogether responsible for the fact that you were reared to hate and fear my name which in modesty I would suggest is not without its own ebullient music. I say further that you too are blind in your way, and now you use me to try to justify that blindness. By your own admission you are empty also. So you invited me to people your emptiness. This I will do without remorse or reward. But kindly remember that you are blind and that I see.

The butcher walked out the door of my emptiness, straight into me.

Balloons

Friends beat me up on the way home from school.
Suddenly, a new time happened in me.
It wasn't that I'd come the rough or acted the fool
Too much for them to bear, it was more that they
Needed a victim that June afternoon
When you had to clamp your mouth against the flies
Cancering the air. Since then, I hate June
Because both my hips, under the bruises,
Stopped growing. In the orthopaedic hospital
I'm in the next bed to this Indian
Who can hardly be moved but a bone breaks;
My moon-faced brother looms, his pockets all
Balloons. Weights on my legs, promising man-
hood, suggesting they're the colours of mistakes.

The Ceiling

The way it leaned down on me then I felt
Like a pound note pressed inside a wallet.
I might be used to thin somebody's guilt
Or dropped in a collection to buy bullets
And bombs for those in need of such noises.
Higher up, swallows are making brief homes.
I have never seen mud put to such use.
These builders will fly away from their ruins
And I'll be left, like winter, doubting
The heart of all stabs at architecture,
My own being happily laughable.
If I take it on me to get a house moving
Ceilings will be high as thoughts of disaster,
Unpressing, might as well not be there at all.

The Curse

The first time I heard the curse in sleep
Was now and a thousand years ago
It didn't assume a pig-shape or dog-shape
Nor was it tarred and feathered like a crow
It wasn't an old soldier talking his wounds
Nor a priest going fifteen rounds with the Devil
It wasn't the smell of blood in killing hands
I'd hardly call it foul

It was more like a small patient hiss
The sound a wind might make trying to be born
A kind of pleading
                    the let-me-have-my-way
Of a child who gets a notion in his
Head to go somewhere
                    only to return
With words like 'I'm back now I want to stay'.

Oliver to His Brother

Loving brother, I am glad to hear of your welfare
And that our children have so much leisure
They can travel far to eat cherries.
This is most excusable in my daughter
Who loves that fruit and whom I bless.
Tell her I expect she writes often to me
And that she be kept in some exercise.
Cherries and exercise go well together.
I have delivered my son up to you.
I hope you counsel him; he will need it;
I choose to believe he believes what you say.
I send my affection to all your family.
Let sons and daughters be serious; the age requires it.
I have things to do, all in my own way.
For example, I take not kindly to rebels.
Today, in Burford Churchyard, Cornet Thompson
Was led to the place of execution.
He asked for prayers, got them, died well.
After him, a Corporal, brought to the same place
Set his back against the wall and died.
A third chose to look death in the face,
Stood straight, showed no fear, chilled into his pride.
Men die their different ways
And girls eat cherries
In the Christblessed fields of England.
Some weep. Some have cause. Let weep who will.
Whole floods of brine are at their beck and call.
I have work to do in Ireland.

In Dublin

'Swearing, cursing, fighting, drunkenness,
God's Holy Name dishonoured and blasphemed
To the scandal and grief of all good men,
Obscenity the Devil would be hard put to dream,
Nothing but contempt for the laws of the land
And the known articles of war –
I will change the ways of this reeking town
For the good of the Irish poor:

Let the buff coat, instead of the black gown
Appear in Dublin pulpits; God knows it is
Meritorious to use two swords well.
Silence St Austin and Thomas Aquinas,
Let Protestant honesty come into its own.'

He stabled his horses in St Patrick's Cathedral.

Manager, Perhaps

The first time I met Oliver Cromwell
The poor man was visibly distressed.
'Buffún' says he, 'things are gone to the devil
In England. So I popped over here for a rest.
Say what you will about Ireland, where on
Earth could a harassed statesman find peace like
This in green unperturbed oblivion?
Good Lord! I'm worn out from intrigue and work.
I'd like a little estate down in Kerry,
A spot of salmon-fishing, riding to hounds.
Good Lord! The very thought makes me delighted.
Being a sporting chap, I'd really love to
Get behind one of the best sides in the land.
Manager, perhaps, of Drogheda United?'

A Language

I had a language once.
I was at home there.
Someone murdered it
Buried it somewhere.
I use different words now
Without skill, truly as I can.
A man without a language
Is half a man, if he's lucky.

Sometimes the lost words flare from their grave
Why do I think then of angels,
Seraphim, Cherubim, Thrones, Dominions, Powers?
I gaze amazed at them from far away.
They are starting to dance, they are
Shaping themselves into vengefully beautiful flowers

A Bad Time

Having butchered everyone in the church
The soldiers explore the vaults underneath
Where the choicest ladies are hidden
Hoping to cheat the general death.
One of these, a most handsome virgin,
Kneels down to Thomas à Wood, with prayers
And tears, that he may spare her life.
Sudden pity; he takes her in his arms
Out of the church, intending her escape.
A soldier sees this and pikes her through.
À Wood, seeing her gasping, takes her money
And jewels, flings her down over the works.
Massacre flows for five days in succession.
A bad time for virgins, local people say.

Birthmark

'A gentleman of the troop of the Boyles
Dropped in and cut griskins or collops
Of William Stewart alive;
Stuffing fire-coals into his mouth
He ripped up his belly
Wrapped his entrails about his neck.
It was grisly to see
And yet in all this chopping of Mr Stewart
I was struck by one quiet detail
As people sometimes are
In the midst of howling scenes;
A birthmark on his left breast
Shaped like a broken star.'

Rebecca Hill

Half-hanging is the rage in Kildare
It is the rebels' will
So died Jonas Wheeler William Dandy James Benn
Rebecca Hill

Rebecca Hill was fifteen years
Half-hanged then taken down
As comely a girl as ever walked
Through Kildare Town

Taken half-hanged from an oak tree
She seemed to recover her wits
The rebels saw her flutter alive
Then buried her quick

Leaves of the oak tree still
Mutter like Rebecca Hill.

Some People

Elizabeth Birch had a white neck
They roped it
George Butterwick of the strong body
Looked awkward naked
Sylvanus Bullock liked riding the highway
Died stripped in a ditch
John Dawling a brave swimmer
Drowned thrown off Belturbet bridge
George Netter a providing father
Perished with his five starved children
Philip Lockington a big farmer
Was flogged to an idiot beggar
Oliver Pinder offered shelter to people of the road
His house was pulled down over his head

May the Lord have mercy on the dead.

An Expert Teacher

'God's ways need not be justified' Oliver said.
'Protestants were massacred in 1641.
Those who might have made an Assembly of Saints died
By drowning, fire, strangling, sword and gun.
God ordained they be avenged.
At Drogheda, I saw His judgment executed
Upon these barbarous wretches
Whose hands were thick with innocent blood.
As well as that, God's judgment meant
Less blood would be shed in the future.
The sword is an expert teacher
Like a drowning cry or the smell of burning.
Blood shed in proper quantities prevents
More shedding. Men are quick at learning.'

Such a State

I have seen my friends in some very
Embarrassing positions, and my heart
Which is not sacred has bled for them
Albeit not at a rapid rate, and privately.
But I will never forget the sight
Of Oliver Cromwell in William Street,
Listowel. He was covered in shite.
I was struck dumber than usual. How greet
An old acquaintance in this public place
And he in such a state? No words that I
Could summon would have, at that moment, sufficed.
But then, from somewhere in Oliver's face,
Explanation dropped as from an addled sky:
'Buff, I have been floundering in the bowels of Christ.'

Master

'I am master of the chivalric idiom' Spenser said
As he sipped a jug of buttermilk
And ate a quaite of griddle-bread.
'I'm worried, though, about the actual bulk
Of *The Faerie Queene*. She's growing out
Of all proportions, in different directions.
Am I losing control? Am I buggering it
All up? Ruining my best intentions?
As relief from my Queene, I write sonnets
But even these little things get out of hand
Now and then, giving me a nightmare head.
Trouble is, sonnets are genetic epics.
Something in them wants to grow out of bounds.
I'm up to my bollox in sonnets' Spenser said.

Reading Aloud

Oliver Cromwell is a cultured man
Though he's not fond of the drama.
'Buffún' he said 'I once read all *The Faerie Queene*
Or, to be more precise, I tried to.
Spenser had a little estate down in Cork
And he found peace there, deep, unending,
Like his poem. But think of all the work
He put for years into these singing
Stanzas. That poem is one of England's glories.
Few Englishmen bother to read it now
Though much of it is still fresh as a berry
On a hedge in the middle of the Maharees.
I plan to spend next winter reading it aloud
To myself in my little estate down in Kerry.'

A Relationship

'Cromwell' I said, 'If our relationship
Is to develop, there's something I must tell
You, something from which I can't escàpe.
I hate and fear you like the thought of hell.
The murderous syllables of your name
Are the foundation of my nightmare.
I can never hate you enough. That is my shame.
Every day I pray that I may hate you more.
A fucked-up Paddy is what I am. Right?
Wrong. My loathing is such I know
I'll never rest.'

Oliver smiled. I sympathise with your plight,
Buffún. Understandable. You're fine, though, so
Long as you get it off your chest.'

'You really are an understanding
Son-of-a-bitch, Oliver' I replied
'And when this nightmare is over
And I understand why I have hated
You, your language, your army and your Christ
Who suffers your puritan crap
When he should bleed your guts into the sun
Or rip your heart out or break your neck
Or manacle you forever to a rock
Or stuff the barrel of a gun
Up your arse or assassinate your prick

Then we shall sit together
Outside a pub on a June afternoon
Sipping infinite pints of cool beer.
I have been brooding on this, mulling it over,
Our destinies are mingled, late and soon.
But the prospects are not good, I fear.'

Volleys

It was a peaceful September night. All that day
People were talking about the apple crop.
At ten o'clock a car load of detectives drove into the place,
Halted in the square, confabbed, looked up
And down the streets, began to question the villagers,
Searched their pockets, smelled their breath, ordered them to wait
Then go straight home. They were to lock their doors
And no matter what happened not to venture out.

Out in the fields the smell of apples sweetened the night air,
There was no thwarting that crop now, summer had kept its promise.
The detectives stood alone in Main Street.
They got into the car, started to drive away.
From the west side of the village ten shots spat out.
It was the second time the volleys were heard that week.

A Running Battle

What are they doing now? I imagine Oliver
Buying a Dodge, setting up as a taxi-driver
Shunting three dozen farmers to Listowel Races.
I see Ed Spenser, father of all our graces
In verse, enshrined as a knife-minded auctioneer
Addicted to Woodbines and Kilkenny beer,
Selling Parish Priests' shiny furniture
To fox-eyed housewives and van-driving tinkers.
William of Orange is polishing pianos
In convents and other delicate territories,
His nose purple from sipping turpentine.
Little island is Big, Big Island is little.
I never knew a love that wasn't a running battle
Most of the time. I'm a friend of these ghosts. They're mine.

Am

When I consider what all this has made me
I marvel at the catalogue:
I am that prince of liars, Xavier O'Grady,
I am Tom Gorman, dead in the bog,
I am Luke O'Shea in Limerick prison,
I sell subversive papers at a church gate,
Men astound me, I am outside women,
I have fed myself on the bread of hate,
I am an emigrant in whose brain
Ireland bleeds and cannot cease
To bleed till I come home again
To fields that are a parody of peace.
I sing tragic songs, I am madly funny,
I'd sell my country for a fist of money
I am a big family,
I am a safe-hearted puritan
Blaming it all on the Jansenists
Who, like myself, were creatures on the run.
I am a home-made bomb, a smuggled gun.
I like to whine about identity,
I know as little of love as it is possible
To know, I bullshit about being free,
I'm a softie crying at the sound of a bell,
I have a tongue to turn snakespittle to honey,
I smile at the themes of the old poets,
Being lost in myself is the only way
I can animate my foolish wits.

Do I believe myself? I spill
My selves. Believe, me, if you will.

*   *   *

A Half-finished Garden

Because her days were making a garden
She haunted that particular beach
Drawing rocks, sticks, shells and stones,
Random-pitched sea-gifts, over the years,
Bog-oak, sculpted and twisted,
She lugged from the beach up to the garden
That was half-finished when she had to leave it
To go to a place of which I know nothing.

Here is the picture (I have nothing but pictures),
The sea helpless to govern its giving
Through rumble and slither, bang, roar and hiss,
A house on a cliff-top with staring blue windows
And, work of the dead to pleasure the living,
A half-finished garden, epitaph, promise.

A Restoration

Was it the lazy haze of the summer afternoon
Drifting into her, or the warm
Indolence of the sea caressing every bone
That made her stretch out on the sandy grass
And give herself into the arms
Of this prolonged, seductive moment?
Was she free a while of children's cries
Boring through her, shrill and insistent?
Whatever it was, she suddenly knew she was naked
And glancing at her left hand
Saw her marriage ring was missing.
She was panic as she searched and searched
Until she found it in the thieving ground
And restored it to its mark, dark and shining.

I See You Dancing, Father

No sooner downstairs after the night's rest
And in the door
Than you started to dance a step
In the middle of the kitchen floor.

And as you danced
You whistled.
You made your own music
Always in tune with yourself.

Well, nearly always, anyway.
You're buried now
In Lislaughtin Abbey
And whenever I think of you

I go back beyond the old man
Mind and body broken
To find the unbroken man.
It is the moment before the dance begins,

Your lips are enjoying themselves
Whistling an air.
Whatever happens or cannot happen
In the time I have to spare
I see you dancing, father.

A Cry for Art O'Leary

(from the Irish of Eibhlín Dubh Ní Chonaill)

My love
The first time I saw you
From the top of the market
My eyes covered you
My heart went out to you
I left my friends for you
Threw away my home for you

What else could I do?

You got the best rooms for me
All in order for me
Ovens burning for me
Fresh trout caught for me
Choice meat for me

In the best of beds I stretched
Till milking-time hummed for me

You made the whole world
Pleasing to me

White rider of love!

I love your silver-hilted sword
How your beaver hat became you
With its band of gold
Your friendly homespun suit
Revealed your body
Your pin of glinting silver
Glittered in your shirt

On your horse in style
You were sensitive pale-faced
Having journeyed overseas

The English respected you
Bowing to the ground
Not because they loved you
But true to their hearts' hate

They're the ones who killed you
Darling of my heart

My lover
My love's creature
Pride of Immokelly
To me you were not dead
Till your great mare came to me
Her bridle dragging ground
Her head with your startling blood
Your blood upon the saddle
You rode in your prime
I didn't wait to clean it
I leaped across my bed
I leaped then to the gate
I leaped upon your mare
I clapped my hands in frenzy
I followed every sign
With all the skill I knew
Until I found you lying
Dead near a furze bush
Without pope or bishop
Or cleric or priest
To say a prayer for you

Only a crooked wasted hag
Throwing her cloak across you

I could do nothing then
In the sight of God
But go on my knees
And kiss your face
And drink your free blood

My man!
Going out the gate
You turned back again
Kissed the two children
Threw a kiss at me
Saying 'Eileen, woman, try
To get this house in order,
Do your best for us
I must be going now
I'll not be home again.'
I thought that you were joking
You my laughing man

My man!
My Art O'Leary
Up on your horse now
Ride out to Macroom
And then to Inchigeela
Take a bottle of wine
Like your people before you
Rise up
My Art O'Leary
Of the sword of love

Put on your clothes
Your black beaver
Your black gloves
Take down your whip
Your mare is waiting
Go east by the thin road
Every bush will salute you
Every stream will speak to you
Men and women acknowledge you

They know a great man
When they set eyes on him

God's curse on you, Morris,
God's curse on your treachery

You swept my man from me
The man of my children
Two children play in the house
A third lives in me

He won't come alive from me

My heart's wound
Why was I not with you
When you were shot
That I might take the bullet
In my own body?
Then you'd have gone free
Rider of the grey eye
And followed them
Who'd murdered me

My man!
I look at you now
All I know of a hero
True man with true heart
Stuck in a coffin
You fished the clean streams
Drank nightlong in halls
Among frank-breasted women

I miss you

My man!
I am crying for you
In far Derrynane
In yellow-appled Carren
Where many a horseman
And vigilant woman
Would be quick to join
In crying for you
Art O'Leary
My laughing man

O crying women
Long live your crying
Till Art O'Leary
Goes back to school
On a fateful day
Not for books and music

But for stones and clay

My man!
The corn is stacked
The cows are milking
My heart is a lump of grief
I will never be healed
Till Art O'Leary
Comes back to me

I am a locked trunk
The key is lost
I must wait till rust
Devours the screw

O my best friend
Art O'Leary
Son of Conor
Son of Cadach
Son of Lewis
East from wooded glens
West from girlish hills
Where rowanberries grow
Yellow nuts budge from branches
Apples laugh like small suns
As once they laughed
Throughout my girlhood
It is no cause for wonder
If bonfires lit O'Leary country
Close to Ballingeary
Or holy Gougane Barra
After the clean-gripping rider
The robust hunter

Panting towards the kill
Your own hounds lagged behind you
O horseman of the summoning eyes
What happened you last night?
My only whole belief
Was that you could not die
For I was your protection

My heart! My grief!

My man! My darling!

In Cork
I had this vision
Lying in my bed:
A glen of withered trees
A home heart-broken
Strangled hunting-hounds
Choked birds
And you
Dying on a hillside
Art O'Leary
My one man
Your blood running crazily
Over earth and stone

Jesus Christ knows well
I'll wear no cap
No mourning dress
No solemn shoes
No bridle on my horse
No grief-signs in my house
But test instead
The wisdom of the law
I'll cross the sea
To speak to the King
If he ignores me
I'll come back home
To find the man
Who murdered my man

Morris, because of you
My man is dead

Is there a man in Ireland
To put a bullet through your head

Women, white women of the mill
I give my love to you
For the poetry you made
For Art O'Leary
Rider of the brown mare
Deep women-rhythms of blood
The fiercest and the sweetest
Since time began
Singing of this cry I womanmake
For my man

bridge

and in the dark to lean across
like a bridge over a river on whose bed
stones are untroubled by what passes
overhead
and kiss the sleep in your body
with I love you I love you
like currents through my head
that is closer to deep water now
than at any time of the day

*   *   *

from **THE BOOK OF JUDAS** (1991)

prades

ozzie is stonemad about prades
so he say kummon ta belfast
for de 12th an we see de orangemen
beatin de shit outa de drums
beltin em as if dey was katliks' heads

so we set out from dublin
an landed in belfast for de fun
it was brill
dere was colour an music an everyone
was havin a go at sumtin i dunno

what but i'll never forget ozzie in
de middul of all de excitement
pickin pockets right left and centre

on de train back to dublin he was laffin his head
off, dere shud be more fukken prades he said

skool

dis jesus fella sez ozzie who was he
how de fuck do i know sez i
you went ta skool forra bit sez ozzie
didn't learn much dayre sez i

but he died on de cross sez i
for you an for me de teetchur said
what de fuck you talkin about sez ozzie
de man is dead dat's all de man is dead

but everywun sez jesus dis an jesus dat
pay de jesus rent by us a jesus pint
till i get de jesus dole

but who de jesus hell was he sez ozzie
i dunno sez i yoor jesus iggerant sez he
shuv yoor iggerance up yoor bleedin hole

Staring

'He stood at my bedroom door
Put his left forefinger against
The thin mean line of his mouth.
I was staring at a cross that said
      Ssshh!'

A Second's Eternity

Even when he was acting the tough around Jerusalem
He had a good word for the bad women
Who liked him for how he saw them
And talked to them in their poxy dens.

Late at night when the screwing has to start
In the moaning towns, villages and cities
Where a longing prick is a pain in the heart
And no one is near to give you the kiss of life

And you, like him, might be out walking by
A river, staring at lights, thinking of simple misery
And the ubiquitous insult to simple dignity

Then he, like you, sees a dead dog in the street,
Bends down, touches, you believe he sighs
As he looks for a second's eternity through the dead eyes.

My Mind of Questions

Did Jesus have brothers and sisters?
            Did they give him a rough time?
What was it like on a Saturday night
            In the Holy Family home?

Did they mock his God–like talents?
            Laugh at wise things he said?
Did he fight with them for an extra spud
            Or a cut o' brown bread?

Did he have a favourite sister
            Who understood him better than most
And agreed that he was the Father
            Son and Holy Ghost?

If challenged, would he fight back,
            Square up to a bully?
Was he a handy lad with the mitts
            Sidestepping beautifully

When a bigger lad charged at him,
            Expecting to knock him down?
Did Jesus trip him up
            Then go to town?

What was he like in the scrap
            When the dirt blinded his eyes?
Did he ever get a kick in the balls
            From some frigger twice his size?

When, in the streets of Nazareth,
            Did he first hear the name of God?
Did he know it was his own name
            When he first tasted blood?

Did he go in search of birds' nests
        In meadow, field and glen?
And if he found a thrush's nest
        Did he rob it then?

Did he ever fish for eels
        And watch them die at his feet
Wriggling like love in the dust?
        Gospels, you're incomplete.

What was he like at school?
        Was he fond of poetry?
Did he make the teacher feel like a fool
        Because he lacked divinity?

What did the teacher think of him
        Doing his father's business?
Did he wonder at times if Jesus
        Was out of his tree, or worse?

Did Jesus like to sing?
        Did he whistle and hum
As he walked the streets of Nazareth
        Going home to mum?

(I've heard it said he lacked
        A sense of humour,
That his mind was grim and grew grimmer
        And grimmer and grimmer).

What was his appetite like?
        What did he like to eat?
What did he see the first time he washed
        His hands and feet?

What were his fingers like? His mouth?
        His throat, toes, thighs, teeth, eyes?
Did he often cry? For what? And what
        Was the sound of his sighs

At night when he was alone
   And no one had ever been created
Except as shadowy strangers
   Who went their separate ways?

What did he think of his neighbours?
   His neighbours of him?
Was he a quiet little fella
   Fond of his home?

Or did he sometimes seem
   As if he were biding his time
Like a man with a job to do
   That took up all his mind?

At what moment did he know
   That home is not enough
And he must scour the darkness
   To give and find love

Among strangers waiting out there
   Full of need,
So full his heart inclined
   To bleed?

Did he break up his family?
   Did they resent him?
From the day he left did he ever
   Get in touch again?

Was he handsomely made
   Or humped, mis-shapen?
Was his life a preparation
   For what can never happen?

When he saw the sadness of sex
   Did he sit and think
Or slip down a Nazareth laneway
   For a happy wank?

Back in the Holy Family
        All hope and despair on the shelf
Did he look in the eyes of others
        Or smell himself?

Did he stand in a doorway of time
        Look at a street
Hear people bawl for his blood
        And then forget

He'd ever existed? Did he shudder
        To know the future now?
Did he know? How could he bear it?
        The sweat on the boy's brow

Turns to blood in my mind of questions,
        How foolish they are,
What do I know of anything,
        Even my own star?

My own star above all, perhaps?
        My own blood?
My own tracking, trackless, shapeless, restless,
        Sleepless head?

A Scattering of Hay

I go back to the stable this winter night.
The door coughs open, I edge into the darkness,
Stand still. Somewhere, an old woman
Is shouting in a drunken voice,

      'Every mother's son in this accursed place
Has to go to a foreign country to make a livin'.
This bloody hell is a curse-o'-God disgrace.'

She stops, whimpering. I hear a bottle smashing
Against a wall. My eyes search the darkness.
Opposite me, near a corner, lies a cow,
Sleeping, I think. Men's voices blur from the road.

I move slowly over to where the manger is,
I put my hand in the manger, there's only
A scattering of hay, I feel cold and sad,
The feeling passes, I stand in the dark a while.
Nothing, no sound but the cow's breathing, calm and even.
Men I have drunk and yarned with would smile
To see me here, standing, they'd say, on the floor of heaven.

I Never

I have a taste for Latin since I answered Kelch's Mass,
I loved the bell, the bread of God, I loved the words
Hic est enim calyx sanguinis mei.
The time is now, my head bends towards
White marble and whispers whispers whispers
Eternity breathes like a frosty morning
Kelch lifts the chalice up to heaven's windows
Nothing is stale and faded, all pictures bright and shining

Though Kelch's cough is rattling his throat,
He drinks the wine, wine rattles his Adam's apple,
He swallows God with phlegm, the day is blest,
The calming bell strokes demons out of blood,
I never died or cried or lost, betrayed or was betrayed
Till *Ite, missa est, Ite, missa est.*

The Crossword Man

Bombs have a tricky habit of betraying
The intentions of the bomber despite the purest
Patriotic intentions. This one
Had quite a reputation as a boy
For solving knotty crosswords
In the posh English papers

        But now he's betrayed
By his own home-made creation
    Up to its wicked capers.

Look at Lucy Willowes o no you can't
For she's in pieces in a plastic bag
And the crossword man is gone home

To plan a weekend cooling off in a mountain shack
Clean air clean food clean water he'll be glad he came
To ponder Five Across Seven Down: shake, shade, shape, or shame?

The Experiment

I'm not sure where the experiment began.
Some say it was the brainchild of a traffic-cop
Who developed ideas on the nature of man.
Flanagan says it started in a small room behind a breadshop
Where connoisseurs gathered to sample the baker's best
And measure ways in which bread kept them alive
As much, at least, as milk from a mother's breast.
Hitler, who holds all culture springs from people's fear of the grave,
Believes, if I understand him, the experiment started
At an undertaker's party in an Austrian village
Resonant, on that occasion, with music and song.
      Theories of origins vary, yet all are agreed
Somewhere along the line, for reasons hard to grasp,
The experiment went wrong.

A Potholed Version

Obstacles to conversion are many.
Bringing souls to God is a canny art.
A dedicated lad, I put my heart
Into the job in many's the rough country.

When we were converting Ireland
There was small pleasure, much pain.
Frankly, despite my prayers, fasting, good deeds,
Pilgrimages to bleak centres of penance,
I never grew accustomed to the fuckin' rain.

But worse than that, dear brothers in Christ,
Scattered like mini-abysses throughout the land
Were the Grand Canyon potholes in every road
Gaping like hell's mouths in that boggy sod.

After many broken ankles, cracked shinbones, sprained backs,
We lost
All trust in the inhabitants of the island
And got out fast
To trail elsewhere with the Word of God.

God knows what we left behind.
A potholed version of The Message comes to mind.

The Heads

Look at the heads.
Consider what a night's carousing will reveal:
Grey hair at the temples, mouth half-open
Chest out like a boy's full of pride
Strong fingers caressing a glass into warmth
Legs outstretched, all pain gone for the moment
But it'll be back and that's for certain,
Lips laughing now as they haven't laughed for years.
There will be talk of this night, such talk
It'll scorch the packed wax in their ears.
Look at those eyes, jewels beautifully alone,
That one's right hand under his chin, the light
Quietly fingering his jawbone.
Such a night! All together! Yet each one keeps his place
Including me, there, at the corner, near the end.
You can't define me as enemy or friend.
I've never seen such a determined look on a man's face.

Bed

They wrote me down! The watchers wrote me down!
What sneaking watcher had the gall to write me down?
There are more versions of me than there are judging men.
When the master spoke, he said he was one,
Or three-in-one, or one-in-three, some such drivel.
A few who use words speak heart and soul,
Speak the blood's black skies as far as they're able.
Eat soulwords, heartwords, bloodwords. Or go to the devil.
The devil may not have you, of course, he's very pernickety
About those he's willing to use his words on.
He told me he once spent seven eternities,
Including an eternity chez God, struggling to find his own
Voice. When he did, it surprised even himself
With its infinite range of infernal effect.
His accent is bland, posh, with the occasional
Descent into crude if colourful peasant dialect.
He loathes vulgarity, he suspects it's good for the soul,
He has a liking for Sanskrit and official forms
Of Irish, he gives the nod to Anglo-Saxon's rutting edge,
Milton is his favourite poet, he thinks the Bible is crap,
Forbids his kids to read it, might keep them free from harm
And harm teaches kids the nature of the storm.
Such is the devil's word-mastery, he's turned hell into a college
Where choice language is really on the map.
      The Map of Ireland is what girls making beds in hotels
Dub semen-stains of sleepers on the sheets.
I leave it to you to imagine who makes the devils' beds in hell
And what they call the sheetstains of the devilsleep,
If sleep there be. Who lies in a devil's bed?

Who lies in yours? In yours? Lies, lies, lies,
Who knows the cosy hole where Cain was chosen to be bad?
What was your hot spawning-spot? Or mine?
I flatter myself, a castellated Victorian double-poster,
I'm just joking, y'know, I must, and yet I speculate
(You must too) on the warmth of that populating stink.
Every cretin among us has to come from somewhere,

Trouble starts in bleedin' bed, some usual stupo night,
In the beginning was the word and the word was – well, what
          do you think?
Think! Think until you are a pain-thorned head.
What then? Your favourite pills. Fall into bed.

doorway

why, in that moment
of heart's darkness, of
severance without end,
did you turn to me
in the freezing doorway,
smile and say 'I'll always
be your friend'?

No Exit

You would think, were you given to thought, that
A man on the brink of immortal shame
Might, shocked, falter. I did not.
Instead, as I kissed, I had a quick vision
Of a bungalow two miles the Dublin side
Of Clonmel. There was something Spanish about it,
But parodied, so vulgar it shrieked of the new-moneyed.
I couldn't explain my presence there, I didn't know what
Neighbours I had, or if I had any,
There was no trace of car or bicycle,
Carrots blushed in the garden, I wouldn't starve
Though famine is the least I might be said to deserve,
That bungalow was the ugliest thing ever visual-
ised by the bungalowblissful genius of man,
I would live there forever, no exit, on my own,
My big picture windows facing the road,
A vegetarian recluse with a special knowledge of God,
Planning, on brain-chilling mornings, a beautiful suicide.

Heigh-Ho

Judas Iscariot is buried and dead
Heigh-Ho buried and dead
And the heartbreaking worms work to nibble his head
Heigh-Ho nibble his head

Judas Iscariot has run out of cash
Heigh-Ho run out of cash
O give him a choice of the nail or the lash
Heigh-Ho the nail or the lash

Judas Iscariot has run out of hope
Heigh-Ho run out of hope
And he's casting his eye on this rogue of a rope
Heigh-Ho this rogue of a rope

Judas Iscariot would make a great cry
Heigh-Ho make a great cry
But he knows in his heart he'd get no reply
Heigh-Ho get no reply

Judas Iscariot with silence is one
Heigh-Ho silence is one
Questions and answers can't tell what is done
Heigh-Ho tell what is done

Judas Iscariot swings from a tree
Heigh-Ho swings from a tree
O he was the bad one the good ones agree
Heigh-Ho the good ones agree

Judas Iscariot grins at his doom
Heigh-Ho grins at his doom
Where did he come from? Out of what womb?
Heigh-Ho out of what womb?

Judas Iscariot is hanging alone
Heigh-Ho hanging alone
And no one can say where Judas is gone
Heigh-Ho Judas is gone

But I met an old goat who said Judas is well
Heigh-Ho Judas is well
And as long as that's true there's hope left in hell
Heigh-Ho there's hope left in hell

Things I Might Do

I thought of things I might do with my heart.
Should I make it into a month like October,
A chalice for the sad madness of leaves
That I might raise in homage to the year's end?

Should I make it into a small white church in
A country-place where bells are childhood prayers?
Or a backroom of a brothel in Dublin
Where the trade of somethinglikelove endures?

Should I make it a judge to judge itself?
Or a caring face in a memory-storm?
Or a bed

For Judas dreaming of the tree :
    'There now, there now, rest as best you can,
    Darling, rest your treacherous head
    And when you've rested, come home to me.'

Last Moments

Wars before and after
Howl through the last moments of my silver laughter.

Comment

How could she know, that girl from the hot
Village at the edge of the legend-lake
Deep and rippling through her childhood
The ebb and flow of every give and take

Among parents sisters brothers and the one
For whom she knew that she'd give all
And all would never be enough, she thought;
Caring him when his day's work was done,

How could she know, opening under him
One sharp March night of witnessing stars
And the occasional slouching cloud

That in her body was the tame
Beginning of the man whose name still stirs
Comment for the way he treated God?

poemprayer

he escaped then from the prison of his body
out into the decent air
leaving behind the pathetic rubbish
that was all right in its own way
and he made a poem to his Lady
that was a true and beautiful prayer

this poem was made out of all his longings
scattered like shells and stones on the shore
it was made of moments after lies were told
and he feared love might be no more
it was made of words lost at night and the tired eyes of women
and shadows gadding on the kitchen floor

it was made of moments of betrayal and wonder
and mockery and slander and pain
it was made of dead friends and enemies
and stories of this man and that woman
it was made of every defeat he had faced or ignored
and hurts known and unknown

today i heard an old man say the poemprayer
in a clear strong voice
that turned this battered world for a moment
into a warm-hearted house
and the clouds of heaven and the stones of the road
were glad to rejoice

*   *   *

A Great Day

She was all in white.

Snow
Suggests itself as metaphor

But since this has been so often said
I may be justified in considering it dead.
Something about snow is not quite right.

Therefore, she was all in white.

He was most elegant too
All dickied up in dignified blue.

They came together, as is habitual
In that part of the world,
Through a grave ritual,

Listening
With at least a modicum of wonder –
What God has joined together
Let no man put asunder.

Man in woman, woman in man.
Soon afterwards, the fun began.

It was a great day –
Long hours of Dionysiac festivity.

Songs poured out like wine.
Praises flowed as they had never done.

The people there
Seemed to see each other in a new way.
This added to the distinction of the day.

And all the time she was all in white
Enjoying every song and speech
Enjoying every sip and every bite.

Such whiteness seems both beautiful and true
He thought, all dickied up in dignified blue.

He looks so good in blue
(This warmed her mind)
Blue suits him
Down to the ground.

At the table where they sat
Things seemed to fit.

And the loud crowd sang and danced
The whole day long, the whole night long.
There could never be anything but dance and song.

I must change, she whispered,
I must change my dress.

He never saw the white dress again.

In the train, the trees wore their rainy veils
With a reticent air.

It's good to get away, she whispered,
Touching her beautiful hair.

She closed her eyes, the trees were silent guests,
A tide of thoughts flowed in her head,
In his head.

'Darling, it was a great day,' she said.

Fragments

What had he to say to her now?
Where was the woman he believed he had known
In a street, out walking, by the sea,
In bed, working, dancing, loving the sun

And saying so, always for the first time?
Who was this stranger with the graven face?
What led to the dreaming-up of a home?
And what was he, at sixty? Who was

That man lifting the blackthorn stick
With the knobbed top from its place
At the side of the fire, quietly dying?

He listened to his own steps in the walk
Past the reedy mud where plover rose
And scattered, black fragments, crying.

Santorini

(for Michael, Edna and Sarah Longley)

In this volcanic, dreaming place
Six Greek poets
Resurrect my mother's face
And set my father dancing again
As if death had never happened.

    Nikos, Yannis, Stella,
    Liana, Demosthenes, John

Smile as the Blasket Islanders
Make love to the sandwomen.
They grapple with my daughter's questions –
What happens all the flowers? What happens all the people?
And when a memory shivers
With images of love and loss
And Yannis asks 'What is this pain?'
I live it all again
And learn once more to let it go
As the people of this island
Living with their volcano
      Muttering rumbling threatening
Take their daily lives in their hands
And go on making wine
And baking bread.
I'll take two volcanic stones
And put Atlantis in my pocket.
When will this earth explode again?

    Liana, Demosthenes, John,
    Stella, Yannis, Nikos,

Your precise fire will sing for me
In my explosive country
And when I look into your book
A small boat making a huge V

In that blue sea will astonish me
With gratitude.

      I touch the stones.
My mother smiles, my father dances,
My daughter peppers me with questions,
A swimmer finds his music, an ambulance screams
In mercy, I build a bridge of love,
The willow speaks, the lightning dreams,
The blackbird sings, I make a wish, the gift appears
To bless this art
        that deepens friendship
           through the years.

*   *   *

from **POETRY MY ARSE** (1995)

Friend

' 'Tis only an old skull,' said Ace, 'that once
        contained ideas, music, song.
Nothing to fear from it, I'd rather have it for a friend
        than many a living tongue.'
I looked at the skull: old gasgob, eyehole, greybone.
        My own.

The cries of time

Why Ace left the house in the suburbs
with the woman standing at the door
bidding him farewell, a serious farewell
believing he was going nowhere
since that's what their attempts to live
together proved beyond all doubt to her

will not be stated here, let alone explored
(certain forms of agony leave everybody bored).
But leave he did, to find the Bluebell Pad,
walks by the Liffey of death and love
and rambling chats with Lucifer and God.

Such ramblings! Such wanderlust of mind!
Up and out in the dripping middle of the night,
wandering through the Phoenix Park
that he might contemplate the Dublin light.

Once, as he strolled the midnight gloom
he heard cries he'd never heard before.
His whole world became a tiny room
and all the cries lived in his blood and bones.

Cries of animals he'd heard, cries of birds,
of children, beaten women, hunger-cries,
cries of silent pain, voices on the phone,
cries of girls fucked by lies,
cries of old men ditched in homes for nobody,
cries of women who have seen through men
or haven't, cries of poverty, of money,
cries of lovers knowing love won't come again.

But the cries of time proclaimed themselves the cries of time
and nothing more. How so? It was the way
they cried for all things but themselves,
all hearts, especially those with nothing to say.

Like Ace's heart that night not long ago, or long ago.

Nothing to say. Nor did Ace try to say
anything but shambled through the darkness
till he came to the river shambling to the sea.

What have you to say, river? What have you to say to me?

For a while, again, Ace was ice. How long
in God's name would it take him to melt
back to mankind? That's the beauty of walking
through night, that slow sense of melting without guilt,
the search for weariness, the dream of sleeping
if not in a lover's arms, well then, alone,
the pillow blood-spotted, the dream beginning,
the cries of time trapped in a sleeping man
and who knows the gifts and griefs of morning?

By fire and quayside

How was I to know the sadness would return
to numb my body, drown my mind
when you stood by the fire after twenty years
and laughed, and spoke words near and kind
as the woman's by the quayside when she said
'Bit o' love, love? Now. Twenty quid.'

Home and away

Ace is living me today.
He's at home now, I've slipped away.
Who is saying whatever there's to say?
Who dares shape the curse? Who dares pray?

Letter to Ace: I want to tell the robins

'The robins are playing on the bridge today.

That mad March light gave me courage to face the fear
of seeing a fool reflected in the mirror.
   The air whispered to me –

             "Yerra, fuck it,
which is better: being nothing at all
or a gadabout fool?"

The sun kissed my skin, I felt a smile
playing on my face.
      I was new.
      I believed in my own style.

I want to tell the robins
about your laughter, your words
opening these windows,
            making me new,
     kissed by the sun
as I'd never been kissed by a man.

     You're gone
        and yet
            you live in me,

  old man, old poet, old busy bee,
you gave me treasure that you'll never see.'

Blasting away

Ace is blasting away at his Europoem
poem to Homer Goethe Dante Camoëns Shakespeare
Blake, all the voices of obscure parishes
burdened with universality

His mind streels down a street in Portugal
pauses at a shrine in southern Spain
dips into a well-lit brothel in Berlin
suffers the dreary spits of Irish rain

Europoem is flaking right ahead
Ace is a map of that bashed old place
all the voices of the articulate dead
co-light to fight mind's darkness in his face

Blitzed-ignorant, three things he loves: gumption, gaiety, grace.

Her father

'I walked with my father
   to Adam and Eve's
every Sunday morning
   through the city of Dublin

my father showed me
   God's grief and tears
I gave to heaven
   my small prayers

while outside the river
   flowed like the days
and inside the church
   the people sang praise

to the God beyond pain
   Whom we asked to come
like the light of dawn
   into our hearts
with his bread of love.'

Everything Molly said

Molly the waitress asked me, 'What's up
with your man, Ace de Horner?
He thinks he's a genius, he thinks he's
doin' you a favour when he says good mornin',

he thinks his shit is ice-cream.
O pardon me, sir, that just popped out,
don't worry, it'll pop back in.
But why does Ace de Horner walk about
with a dog as ugly as Original Sin?

Kanooce is the dog's name, sir. Funny name. Kanooce.
But Jesus, sir, that dog would ate
a farmer's arse though a hedge.

Kanooce's jaws are always drippin' juice
like blood, or blood like juice. Sooner or later,
he'll gobble a tinker on O'Connell Bridge
or some poor soul in Westmoreland Street.
And what will Ace de Horner do about that?'
'I don't know,' I replied, 'I just don't know'.

Molly was worried. Then she said
'Mr de Horner is always talkin' about the poetic art
but the world would be a safer place
if poets and killerdogs were kept apart.
Would you tell that to the Taoiseach, sir,
or write a letter to the paper?'

'I'll convey your message to the Arts Council,'
I replied, 'I'll tell them all you've said,
down to the last word.'

I did. I received, after two months, a note
pulsating with gratitude, ending with
'We'll take everything that Molly said on board.'

The soul's loneliness

it's nothing to go on about
but when I hear it
in the ticking of the clock

beside the books and photographs
or see it in the shine
of an Eason's plastic bag at midnight

or touch it in the tree I call
Christ there outside my window
swaying in the day's afterglow

I shiver a little at the strangeness
of my flesh, the swell of sweat,
the child's poem I'll never forget

and find my eyes searching the floor
for a definition of grace
or a trace of yourself I've never noticed before.

Down

why does a poem
always
go
down
the page
like
a shooting
star
or a spade
cutting
into earth
making way
for seeds
to nestle
in darkness
and slowly
begin
to become
(for example)
a small
white
flower
perfect
in the
light?

*   *   *

from **THE MAN MADE OF RAIN** (1998)

[28]

Major operations on the body
operate the mind.

At twenty past four
the goddesses let their waters flow.
Stories of long ago.

The black bar ramming three white clouds
is a wound gone underground.

Up on the ditch he set me
when I was nine,
stuck his hand up my trousers,
his black eyebrows scorching me
his tongue licking his turfy lips.

'Did you bring me any black Bendigo tobacco?' he asks.
'I love it, 'tis the devil to cut though I have
the wickedest little knife in the world.'

His hands are calm and mad.
Sit still on the ditch, don't scream,
his black eyebrows fester with rats.

Paddy Brolley traps me between his legs.
He's eighty years of age, I'm eight,
he's laughing, his knees bang me,
manipulating,
coddin' is what he'll call it
if I start screaming.

'Now I have you trapped.
You'll never escape.'

More than half a century later
I'm trapped between his legs.

His old penis twitches like a rat in his grey trousers.

His laughter is a cage as well.
Paddy Brolley is a bit o' hell,
the bones of his knees are digging into my eyes
my mind is bleeding, he's laughing, why
is blood always surprising,
is the pillow drenched, are the feathers protesting?

What can I do
but let blood flow
like memories of long ago
that are the living now,
madcap antics, love, hate, rage,
rob Collins's orchard, run, hide, eat
the apples under the bridge, quick,
there's a comin' tide.

Tonight, I'm trapped in a cage.

No coddin'.

Mindbleeding never ends.

What's half a century between friends?

Now is then, then is now,
no such thing as long ago.

In the stillness of the night
in the prone silence of the body
I know
the fierce uncontainable flow
of the gentle eyes
of the man of rain.

It is part of me tonight,
this high springtide of blood
lifting in its rising hands
images

I cannot hide.

How much have I hidden?

How much have I lied?

Give me the courage
to rise and flow with the tide.

I can't see him but I know
he's standing out there
in here
in the darkness
in my mind

at my side.

*　　*　　*

Saint Brigid's Prayer

(from the Irish)

I'd like to give a lake of beer to God.
    I'd love the Heavenly
Host to be tippling there
    for all eternity.

I'd love the men of Heaven to live with me,
    to dance and sing.
If they wanted, I'd put at their disposal
    vats of suffering.

White cups of love I'd give them
    with a heart and a half;
sweet pitchers of mercy I'd offer
    to every man.

I'd make Heaven a cheerful spot
    because the happy heart is true.
I'd make the men contented for their own sake.
    I'd like Jesus to love me too.

I'd like the people of Heaven to gather
    from all the parishes around.
I'd give a special welcome to the women,
    the three Marys of great renown.

I'd sit with the men, the women and God
    there by the lake of beer.
We'd be drinking good health forever
    and every drop would be a prayer.

*   *   *

At home

Love soars and dips
like the first swallow
at home in exile
over Doran's meadow.

Scratchword

The word is scratched on a small stone
in the shadow of a rock:
epic.

Home

'No place like home,' she said,
    eighty in her rocking chair
'where you can spit in the fire
    saucer your tea
        and call the cat a bastard.'

Shaper

I love the strange men and women
arranged on the shelf
but there's no stranger like the stranger
shaping the self.

Up from the earth

Up from the earth the voices came,
        voices buried stripped years ago
singing weeds and grass, gravel and bones,
        lovers I cannot begin to know.

Voices of friends who died in childhood,
        Tommy Brassil of the gentle smile,
Nellie Connor who laughed and vanished
        into the earth in a fevered while.

Up from the earth the voices come,
        glimpses of spirits that live in me.
Why do they suddenly sound, then vanish
        into eternity?

A quick visit

Love dropped in for a quick visit
had a glass of wine and a slice of bread
then faced the road and the night ahead.

Earth and sea

Children screaming in the playful sea
watched by an old man on the clifftop:

old man in the earth, watch over me.

Odyssey

She trudged a long way through mucky fields to feed birds.
She heard them singing afterwards.

Still to be done

Tiredness hits him, failure snuggles in close,
years of work stalk him, bleating
and slipping. One thing he knows, one thing.
Everything is still to be done. Everything.

from **MARTIAL ART** (2003)

December

It's December, presents are lunatics –
spoons, napkins, knives, writing-paper,
classy jars of delicious jam.
I've sent you nothing but my small books,
I must seem tight as a mackerel's arse
on a winter's night, and that's water-tight.
But I despise the treacherous generosity
of presents. Presents are like hooks,
the greedy fish is fooled by the fly he swallows.
In refusing to give presents to rich friends,
the poor man shows true generosity.

Best

My best poem will be one line,
define the void, celebrate oblivion.
I shall write it after a perfect dinner
and many glasses of my favourite wine.

Progress

My friend Pudens is marrying Claudia.
May their marriage be forever blessed.
They are perfectly suited to each other
like the elm and the tender vine

the lotus and the water
the myrtle and the shore
Athenian honey and Massic wine.
May Claudia love Pudens when he's old,
may she seem young and beautiful in his eyes
when youth is far behind her.
May their marriage be a calm progress
towards ever deepening happiness.
When they lie down at night, may darkness bless
        togetherness.

Competition

Thought of a star makes a star of thought.
Poets compete. Poems do not.

Drifters

It tortured me in darkness. I wrote it down.
There. Whatever it is, I suppose it's my own
though it may drift away into another person.
Poems are drifters. A mind is an ocean.

Whenever

Whenever I say a prayer
I know why birds' wings
are loved by the air.

*

He recalls how he thought he'd never hear evil music
but he did, one night, between the sea and the street,
the dull stupid Dresden bombing of the devil's heartbeat.

*

Certain midnight creatures shine in darkness.
Nameless they never vanish but gift their magic,
flying in and out of lonely eyes.

*

Tears in his eyes, the old teacher repeats
the same line to the enchanted young:
'And the birds go to sleep by the sweet wild twist of her song.'

*

He follows a word that follows him.
He's catching up, the word swerves, vanishes
into a swan's wing.

Poem

Most of the time I sing what you'd have me sing,
say what you'd have me say,
but now and then I go wandering
up the hill of shadows, astray

until I find the orphan I first met
sixty years ago. He's wandering too,
looking for his mother, father,
brothers and sisters he might see as true

members of the family he never knew.
He knows he will be searching forever,
like me. We talk, then go our ways.
I pause at the bottom of the hill where

the river flows like the poem I may
become. But who knows in whose heart
I may be born? Old man's? Young woman's?
Brain-damaged prisoner's? Who will say I'm art?

I look back, up. Where is the hill of shadows?
Grey clouds cover it. Where is the orphan now?
And who is the person shaping to write me down?
Words are wild creatures. Fly them home.

INDEX

Index of titles

The Essential Brendan Kennelly CD

The CD accompanying *The Essential Brendan Kennelly* draws upon four recordings by Brendan Kennelly. Any poems included in those original recordings which were selected by the editors for this book are included on the CD. The numbers in square brackets are the page numbers of those poems. The other poems can all be found in *Familiar Strangers: New & Selected Poems 1960-2004* (Bloodaxe Books, 2004), except for the translation, 'The Old Woman of Beare', which is in *Love of Ireland: poems from the Irish* (Mercier Press, 1999).

TRACKS 1-7: *Living Ghosts: 23 Poems* (cassette, Livia Records, 1982), recorded in 1982 at the Centre for Language and Communication Studio, Trinity College Dublin and produced by Gerald Davis.

TRACKS 8-18: *The Poetry Quartets 4* (cassette, Bloodaxe Books/British Council, 1999), recorded on 23 June 1999 at Trinity College Dublin and produced by Felicity Goodall. This is the complete recording of Brendan Kennelly's reading from a double cassette shared with Paul Durcan, Medbh McGuckian and Michael Longley.

TRACKS 19-32: *Brendan Kennelly reading from his poems* (CD, The Poetry Archive, 2002), recorded in June 2002 by Audio-Visual & Media Services, Trinity College Dublin and produced by John Rowland. Thanks are due to Richard Carrington and The Poetry Archive for their kind permission.

TRACKS 33-37: *The Man Made of Rain* (cassette, Bloodaxe Books, 1998), recorded in February 1998 by Audio-Visual & Media Services, Trinity College Dublin and produced by John Rowland.

LIVING GHOSTS (1982)

1: Living Ghosts [57]
2: The Gift [20]
3: The Swimmer
4: The Thatcher
5: The Pig-killer [34]
6: The Gift Returned
7: The Old Woman of Beare

THE POETRY QUARTETS: 4 (1999)

8: Poem from a Three Year Old [54]
9: The Visitor [51]
10: My Dark Fathers [26]
11: 'Therefore, I Smile' (from *Cromwell*)
12: Am (from *Cromwell*) [88]
13: Dream of a Black Fox [37]
14: Bread [39]
15: Street corner (from *Poetry My Arse*)
16: The Dinner (from *The Book of Judas*)
17: We Are Living
18: I See You Dancing, Father [92]

THE POETRY ARCHIVE (2002)

19: Getting Up Early [28]
20: The Singing Girl Is Easy in Her Skill [56]
21: Saint Brigid's Prayer [147]
22: The Horse's Head [61]
23: Love Cry
24: bridge [100]
25: A Restoration [91]
26: A Half-finished Garden [90]
27: A Giving [41]
28: Let It Go [45]
29: Proof
30: A Glimpse of Starlings
31: Clearing a Space
32: Begin [33]

THE MAN MADE OF RAIN (1998)

33: What?
34: Part 1: 'Between living and dying...'
35: Part 22: 'Come into the ground with me now, he says...'
36: Part 28: 'Major operations on the body...' [143]

Many thanks to Dave Maughan at Face Musical Productions for his expert sound engineering work on this CD.